The Gos

The Gospel
of Mark

Translated by
Kalmia Bittleston

Floris Books

First published by Floris Books in 1986

British Library Cataloguing in Publication Data

Bible. N.T. Mark. *English. Bittleston. 1986*
The Gospel of Mark.
I. Bittleston, Kalmia
226'.3052   BS2583

ISBN 0–86315–038–1

Printed in Great Britain
by Billing & Sons Ltd, Worcester

Contents

Acknowledgement

The publication of this book has been assisted in memory of Ray Harrison, and in gratitude for her help in preparing it.

Preface

In order to understand something, it must be necessary to know it, and the better it is known the more it should be understood.

This certainly also applies to the Gospels, and yet, throughout the centuries, people who have studied them closely appear to have reached very different conclusions. Theologians and commentators could certainly not be accused of lack of knowledge of the text, but nevertheless have been quite able to select quotations which they felt supported their own beliefs. Belief leads to action, as in the great controversy between the Church authorities, including the rich and powerful Benedictine Order, and the Franciscans, which came to its climax early in the fourteenth century. They disagreed about the poverty of Christ. Did he own property, and should his followers do so? In practice prelates and abbeys became even more magnificent, while bare-footed friars roamed the countryside begging. Some were even regarded as dangerous revolutionaries, and found themselves in prison, while others were burned to death as heretics.

With the rise of Bible criticism arguments tended to be about the historical background of the Gospels, and the relationship of Christ Jesus to his mission. Did he himself claim to be the Messiah? Often everything in the Gospels which seemed to be outside everyday experience was simply regarded as myth.

Today this attitude remains on the one hand; while on the other there is action on behalf of the poor, supported by liberation theology.

The question then remains—how can the Gospel be read, not to support a particular point of view, but to find the truth which is there.

No one can hope to find more than a few aspects of this truth, remembering that truth is as wide as the universe but has an individual aspect for every human being. It is a first step to try to see one of the Gospels as a whole. This is quite difficult with Mark. A great number of events appear before the inner eye of the reader. Some are described in vivid detail, others more briefly, but it all goes very quickly. One of Mark's favourite words can be translated as 'immediately', 'at once', or in the Authorised Version, 'straightway'. It may be necessary to make a conscious effort to slow down, and notice particularly those verses, easily overlooked, which give important indications about place and time.

Mark has his own music. If John is the strings of the orchestra, Luke the woodwind, Matthew the brass, then Mark is the percussion. According to tradition, he was writing in Rome, and his Gospel has something of the steady forward march of the Legions, along the straight roads to the most distant outposts. The message was indeed carried 'from the East as far as the West', but only entered people's lives in as much as they could receive it. This is still true. What is needed are the eyes to see and the ears to hear.

Kalmia Bittleston

Introduction

There is no single way of approaching the Gospels. Like all spiritual documents they open up according to the eye of the beholder. None of us has that totally objective eye which would enable us to see directly into the life substance of the Gospel. If we know and accept this fact we shall not be tempted to think that what we have discovered is anything like a whole truth. We must be satisfied with just the little insight that we can manage, knowing that further efforts will add to this in time. As the eye opens, so more can be seen.

All the Gospels are history. They describe events which happened at a certain time and at a certain place. We know a lot about the world of that time. Those were the early years of the Roman Empire, a power which embraced the whole Mediterranean world and which was just establishing a political stability that was to hold for two hundred years. If Rome did not take kindly to Christianity in the early centuries, it did provide a world of free communication which enabled the early Church to establish itself. Mark himself was an active Christian missionary whose mother's house in Jerusalem provided the nascent Church with its early centre.

Palestine was less peaceful than other parts of the Empire because of the uniqueness of the Jews. Their ways made them the odd people out in the whole Empire. They could not be assimilated either politically

11

or religiously as other peoples could and their representatives stood firm against the threat to their traditional
existence. The Pharisees and scribes were teachers and
lawyers, and both taught in the synagogues. They were
defenders of Jewish orthodoxy. The Zealots went
further in engaging actively in political opposition to
the Romans. The Sadducees were a hereditary group of
priests responsible for the Temple who compromised
with the Romans to safeguard their positions and
wealth. Members of all these groups (most of whom
had their representatives in the Sanhedrin, the supreme
Jewish Council) combined to ensure the condemnation
and crucifixion of Christ.

'Apocalypse' was part of the air people breathed. The
saviour of the world was expected, but people had
different ideas as to how he would appear. Tensions and
extreme danger could arise at any moment, particularly
through those who saw the task of the Messiah in
political, not religious terms. This made life difficult for
the occupying Romans who were indifferent to religion
but vitally concerned about politics. The Council
exploited these fears to the full in persuading Pilate to
condemn Christ.

The Gospels are also more than history. While the
events they narrate are firmly rooted in history, the
story that they bring is not tied to time or place but
lives on for all time and for all places. They describe a
course of events which came about when Christ lived
in a human body in this world. We read on the one
hand what that meant for him, what he achieved, what
transformation was brought about by his presence. On
the other hand, we read of what happened to those

around him, in particular to the disciples, people who gave up everything to follow him. In them we see the first archetypal beginning of a striving to become Christian. What took place between Christ and his disciples, between Christ and those he healed and taught, between Christ and those who sought to destroy him, has as much significance today for us as it did for his contemporaries.

Mark's Gospel is the shortest and most dramatic of the four. This concentration gives strength and tension to what is being portrayed. The strokes are bold, the colours vivid, the actions clear-cut and the whole story is set within a disciplined structure.

The quality of Mark's writing is immediately apparent in the way he opens his Gospel. Both Matthew and Luke spend a lot of time describing the human background to the Incarnation while John in his Prologue sets the story in its eternal context. Mark has no introduction of any kind beyond announcing 'The Gospel of Jesus Christ' and proceeds straight into the story of the ministry. Likewise at the end of the Gospel, having come to the Resurrection as the culmination of the story, Mark simply ends his narrative there and then, eschewing the obvious literary need for a rounding off, which the other three evangelists provide. Yet by ending with ' . . . because they were afraid' we are left not only with the mystery but with the very real question as to how humanity will respond to this overwhelming event. Mark indicates that this is for us where the story begins. It was only natural that the other possible endings were provided later, but they all lack just the kind of conviction that is so evident throughout Mark's work.

There is also a clear form to the Gospel. It consists of a short prelude and three main movements, each of which has its own structure.

The prelude (1:1–13) concerns the work of John. He appears characteristically without any explanation about his background as the one who prepares the inner and outer scene for the Christ. Much of what is described about him in the other Gospels is left out: the focus is on the coming of the Christ and his entry into his earthly task.

The first movement (1:14–8:26) describes the ministry in Galilee. It is the time when Christ pours out his power in healing and in teaching. Mark stresses the immediate impact of Christ's life on mankind by placing the healings in the forefront of this part of the Gospel. Only in Chapter 4 do we have concentrated teaching. The structure of this section is quite complex. We can see three different elements:

The first concerns the stages of Christ's relationship to the disciples: their calling (1:14), their appointment (3:13), their sending out (6:7). The inner thread of the story can be seen linking these events together as the beginning of a path of discipleship.

Following this there is a second structural element: a section of the Gospel appears to repeat itself in a sequence of parallel events (6:35–7:37 and 8:1–26) each of which begins with a feeding (the five thousand and the four thousand), then continues with a journey over the lake, a controversy with the Pharisees, a conversation on bread or leaven and concludes with a healing (the man with a speech impediment, and a blind man). An examination is being described here of the different important steps in the path of discipleship. The passage is an example as to how structural elements can lead to an appreciation of what the Gospel is really trying to convey.

The third structural element in this first movement is the division into chapters. Although they were not created by the Evangelist (in fact they were made in medieval times) they are coherent sections, each of which again has its own form. Chapters 2 and 3 both open with healings which embody the substance of each chapter. The healing of the paralytic is followed by an altercation with the Jews whose rules paralyse the unfolding of new creative gifts. The healing in the synagogue of the man with the withered hand is followed by the appointment of the new community which will be committed to the renewal of the spiritual life of humanity. These two chapters, describing the transition from the old to the new then make possible the teaching of Chapter 4 in which the new is described in the three parables of the seed: not the old, fixed word, but one which grows and bears new fruit. This teaching leads to the first crisis for the disciples (storm on the lake), showing their need for more training to cope with the implications of this new life. In the three healings of Chapter 5 content is provided to meet this need, where we enter into the deeper mysteries of Christ's power. Here Mark uncharacteristically takes his time. In Chapter 6 the disciples are sent out and begin to assist the Christ in his work. There are six scenes which are related: the first and the sixth show Christ with the crowd (6:1, 6:53); the second and fifth have Christ with the disciples (6:7, 6:47); the third and fourth tell of the supersensory community, the beheading of John and the feeding of the five thousand (6:14 and 6:30). Again, the inner implications of all this have to be worked through (indicated by the second crisis on the water, at the end of the chapter) and so Chapter 7 once again has to build on the foundations, summed up in the healing at the end where the ears are opened and the tongue is released. There is the constant challenge to throw off the old tutelage of the law and discover that the source of life has to be found within. The final section of this movement repeats this cycle of events in another key, raising the story to the moment when the disciples reach through to a realization, though perhaps not yet on a fully conscious level, of what it is that they are following.

The second movement (8:27–10:52) has one great theme which Christ himself utters three times: the prophecy of the Passion, Death and Resurrection. The great moment of Peter's confession is immediately clouded by the reality of the Messiah's task, and indeed by the task which follows from it for humanity. Each time Christ brings these stern words the disciples are plunged into the abyss, yet each time there is a step forwards. The pain is not suffered in vain. The movement, which even though not lacking in inner drama may be described as the slow one, ends with the final healing in the Gospel: of the blind man at Jericho whose hymnlike first public proclamation of the Messiah not only brings the movement to a majestic close but also mirrors its opening theme, the first personal confession of the Christ by Peter.

The last movement (11–16) then opens with the triumphant fanfare of Christ's entry into Jerusalem, setting the tone and the direction of the final drama. The disciples now recede into the background and

INTRODUCTION

Christ stands alone in the face of the powers of this world. When he is nevertheless with his disciples it is only to emphasize the magnitude of their future task and to prepare them for his own death. Mark describes these events without a hint of emotion. He simply conveys the power that lives in the events themselves.

There is also a form to this whole last part of the Gospel which is similar to the one we saw in Chapter 6. Chapters 11 and 16 have an inner relationship (entry into Jerusalem, and the Resurrection) as do Chapters 12 and 15 (parable of the killing of the heir to the vineyard, and the Crucifixion) and Chapters 13 and 14 (Christ with his disciples: apocalyptic teaching, and the promise in the Last Supper of his abiding presence).

Form in a painting, in music; in architecture, indeed in anything in this world, is an orientation but not yet the substance. But in providing us with such an orientation, form offers us a means of penetrating towards the substance. In the Gospel, too, it can be an orientation which helps to direct our perception towards the ultimate reality that lies at the heart of Christ's work and being.

What then is the underlying approach in Mark?

We may think of Christ's work in differing ways: as a moral teaching, as the supreme example of love and sacrifice, as the revelation of the deepest wisdom. It was all these things and many more. Each Gospel has its own background and purpose, each tends to see a particular aspect or dimension of Christ's work. Thus Matthew sees it in relation to the history of his own people and shows how the particular is transformed by Christ into the universal. Luke sees the aspects of human concern, care, and love, and shows how these are raised to the highest level by the Christ. John penetrates to the sphere, in Christ, where wisdom and love become one. The uniqueness of Mark is his experience of Christ's power of life: not the wisdom, nor the love, nor the moral teaching, but quite simply that source of life in Christ which worked outwardly into his surroundings as the power of healing and which worked inwardly into himself as the power that overcame death. It was in meeting and experiencing this extraordinary power of life that the disciples were confronted by the mystery of the Christ. Mark shows how each step in comprehension had to be gained through profound and, in some cases, unnerving experiences and how even when Christ's glorious power of life had won through to its final fulfilment on earth the disciples had still to start on their own conscious realization of that power in themselves. That, too, is where we stand and that is why the Gospel of Mark can speak to us today.

Michael Tapp

In Galilee

Prophecy

Jerusalem

1 *Prologue*

1 Beginning
The Gospel of Jesus Christ
The Son of God

John the Baptist

2 As Isaiah the prophet
Has written
See how I send out my messenger
Before thy face
Who will make ready thy road

3 *A voice calling in the desert*
Prepare the road for the Lord
Make his paths straight

4 John
The one baptizing
Came into the desert
Preaching a baptism
To change heart and mind
For forgiveness of sins

5 All the country of Judea
And all the people of Jerusalem
Went out to him
And when he baptized them
In the River Jordan
They acknowledged their sins

6 John
Was dressed in camel hair
With a leather belt round his waist
He ate locusts
And wild honey

7 And proclaimed
There is one coming after me
Who is stronger than myself
I cannot stoop down and untie
The thong of his sandals

8 I
I have baptized you in water
But he will baptize you
In Holy Spirit

Jesus is baptized

9 It happened during those days
That Jesus
Came from Nazareth in Galilee
And was baptized by John
In the Jordan

10 And immediately
As he came up out of the water
He saw the heavens rent apart
And the Spirit as a dove
Coming down upon him

11   And there was a voice
        Uut of the heavens
            Thou art my son
            The beloved
            I rejoice in thee

        The Temptation
12   Straight away
        The Spirit drove him out
        Into the desert

13   He was in the desert
        For forty days
        Being tempted by Satan

        He was with the wild creatures
        And the angels served him

        Calling of four disciples
14   After John was arrested
        Jesus came into Galilee
        Proclaiming the Gospel of God
15   And saying
                The right moment is here
                The Kingdom of God
                Has come close
                Change your hearts and minds
                And believe the Gospel

16 As he passed by the Sea of Galilee
He saw Simon
And his brother Andrew
Casting nets into the sea
As they were fishers

17   Jesus said to them
          Come with me
          And I will make you
          Into fishers of men

18 At once
They left their nets
And followed him

19 Going a little further
He saw James
The son of Zebedee
And his brother John
In their boat mending the nets

20 He called to them immediately
And leaving their father Zebedee
In the boat with the hired servants
They went with him

The healing of a demoniac
21 They came to Capernaum
And on the sabbath
He went straight to the synagogue
And taught

22 The people
Were astonished at his teaching
Because he taught them with authority
And not like the scribes

23 In their synagogue
Was a man
Who had an unclean spirit

24 Suddenly he cried out
What is between us and you
Jesus Nazarene
Have you come to destroy us?
I know you who you are
The Holy One of God

25 Jesus spoke sternly to him
And said
Be silenced
And come out

26 After throwing him down
And shouting with a loud voice
The unclean spirit
Came forth out of him

27 They were all astounded
And discussing it among themselves
They said
Is this a new teaching?
He has authority

To command the unclean spirits
And they obey him

28 His fame soon spread everywhere
Through all the Galilean countryside

The healing of Simon's mother-in-law
29 Leaving the synagogue
He went straight to the house
Of Simon and Andrew
With James and John

30 Now Simon's mother-in-law
Was lying ill
Stricken with fever
And straight away
They told him about her

31 He went to her
And taking her hand
He lifted her up
The fever left her
And she served them

Healing and teaching in Galilee
32 When evening came
And the sun had set
They brought to him
All those who were sick
Or possessed by demons

33 And the whole town
Was gathered round the door

34 He healed many people
Who suffered from various complaints
And cast out many demons
He did not allow
The demons to speak
Because they knew him

35 Very early in the morning
While it was still night
He rose up and went out
He went away to a desert place
And prayed there

36 Simon
And those with him
Pursued him

37 When they found him
They said
Everyone is searching for you

38 He said to them
Let us go to other places
And into the neighbouring towns
So that I may also preach there
It was for this
That I came out

39 And he preached in their synagogue
Throughout Galilee
And cast out demons

The healing of a leper
40 A leper came to him
Entreating him
And falling on his knees
He said to him
If it is your will
You have the power
To make me clean

41 Filled with compassion
Jesus stretched out his hand
And touched him
Saying
I will
You shall be clean

42 Instantly
The leprosy left him
And he was cleansed

43 Jesus sent him out at once
With the stern warning
44 See that you
Do not tell anyone anything
But go and show yourself to the
priest

> And offer for your cleansing
> What Moses commanded
> As a testimony to them

45 He went out
And began to talk about it
Spreading the news
So that Jesus
Could no longer enter a town openly
But remained in the desert places
And they came to him
From all directions

2 *The healing of a paralytic*
1 Some days later
He again returned to Capernaum
And when the people heard
That he was at home
2 Such a crowd collected
That there was no more space
Not even round the door
And he preached the Word to them

3 A paralytic was brought to him
Carried by four bearers

4 As they could not reach him
Because of the crowd
They opened up the roof above him
When they had made an opening

They lowered the mat
On which the paralytic was lying

5   When Jesus saw their faith
    He said to the paralytic
      Child
      Your sins are forgiven

6   Some of the scribes
  Were sitting there
  Considering in their hearts
7   Why does he speak in this way?
  He blasphemes
  There is only one
  Who has power to forgive sins
  And that is God

8   Immediately
  Jesus became aware in his spirit
  What they were considering within
    themselves
    And he said to them
      Why are you considering this
      In your hearts?
9   Is it easier
      To say to the paralytic
      Your sins are forgiven
      Or to say
      Get up
      Take your mat
      And walk?

10   Only that you may know
          That the Son of Man
          Has authority on the earth
          To forgive sins

      Then he said to the paralytic
11   To you I say
          Get up
          Take your mat
          And go to your house

12   At once he got up
      And taking his mat
      Went out in front of them all
      So that they were filled with awe
      And praised God
          Saying
              We have never seen such a thing

The calling of Levi
13   Again
      When he went out by the sea
      Crowds came to him
      And he taught them

14   As he was passing by
      He saw Levi
      The Son of Alphaeus
      Sitting in the customs house
          And he said to him
              Follow me

He rose up
And followed him

Eating with outcasts
15 Now it happened
That he was having a meal
In his house
And many tax collectors
And outcasts
Were there with Jesus
And with his disciples
As many followed him

16 When the scribes of the Pharisees
Saw that he was eating
With outcasts
And with tax collectors
They said to his disciples
Why does he eat
With tax collectors
And outcasts?

17 Hearing this
Jesus said to them
Those who have good health
Do not need a doctor
But those who are suffering
I did not come
To call the just
But the outcasts

A question about fasting

18 Now John's disciples
Were fasting
As were those of the Pharisees
    So there were some people
    Who came to him and said
        Why do John's disciples
        And the Pharisee's disciples
        Fast?
        But your disciples
        Do not fast?

19   Jesus said to them
        The bridegroom's attendants
        Are not able to fast
        While the bridegroom is with them

        They cannot fast
        At the time
        When the bridegroom is there
20   But the day will come
        When the bridegroom
        Will be taken from them

        In that day
        They will fast

21   No one
    Sews a patch of untreated cloth
    On to an old cloak
    Or the quality of the new

Will pull away from the old
And the tear will be made worse

22
And no one
Puts new wine
Into old wineskins
Or the wine
Will burst the wineskins
And the wine will be lost
As also the skins
But new wine
Is put into fresh wineskins

In the cornfields on the sabbath
23
It happened
That on the sabbath
He was passing through the cornfields
And his disciples
Began picking the ears of corn
Along the way

24
The Pharisees said to him
See
It is the sabbath
So why are they doing something
Which the law forbids?

25
He said to them
Have you never read
What David did
When he was in need

And was hungry
As were those who were with him?

26 How he entered the house of God
When Abiathar was high priest
And ate the loaves of offering
Which it was unlawful
For anyone to eat
Except the priests
And also gave some
To his companions?

27 And he said to them
The sabbath came into existence
For the sake of man
And not man
For the sake of the sabbath
28 So the Son of Man
Is also Lord of the sabbath

3 *The healing of a man with a useless hand*
1 Again
He went into a synagogue
And a man was there
Whose hand had wasted away

2 They watched him narrowly
To see if he would heal
On the sabbath
So that they could accuse him

3   He said to the man
    With the shrunken hand
        Come up into the centre

4   And he said to them
        Is it lawful on the sabbath
        To do good
        Or to do evil?
        To save soul-bearing life
        Or to kill?

5   He looked round on them
    With anger
    Being saddened
    By their closed hearts and minds
        And said to the man
            Stretch out your hand

    He stretched it out
    And his hand
    Was made good

6   When they went away
    The Pharisees
    Immediately conferred with the Herodians
    As to what could be done against Jesus
    To destroy him

    Crowds come to Jesus for help
7   He departed to the sea
    With his disciples

38

And large numbers of people
Followed him
They came from Galilee
And from Judea
8 And Jerusalem
And Idumea
And beyond the Jordan
And from the country
Round Tyre and Sidon

Such a great many came to him
When they heard
About all that he was doing
9 That he told his disciples
That a little boat
Should remain close at hand
Because of the crowds
Who might press upon him

10 He healed many
And those who were afflicted
Struggled to touch him

11 The unclean spirits
When they perceived him
Fell down in front of him
   And cried out
      You are the Son of God

12 And he ordered them
Not to make him known

39

The calling of the twelve

13 He went up on to the mountain
And called to him
Those whom he wished
And they came to him

14 And he appointed twelve
Whom he could sent out
To preach
15 And with authority
To cast out the demons

16 The twelve
Whom he appointed were
Simon
Whom he also named Peter
17 James the son of Zebedee
And his brother John
Whom he named Boanerges
Which means
Sons of Thunder
18 And Andrew
Philip
Bartholomew
Matthew
Thomas
James the son of Alphaeus
Thaddaeus
Simon the Cananaean
19 And Judas Iscariot
The one who betrayed him

20   Then Jesus entered a house
And such a crowd
Collected again
That they could not even eat their meal

21   Hearing of this
His own people set out
To take charge of him
    Because they said
       He is out of his mind

The scribes accuse him

22   The scribes
Who had come down from Jerusalem
Said
    He is possessed by Beelzebub
    Through the ruler of the demons
    He casts out the demons

23   He called them to him
And speaking to them in parables
    He said
      How can Satan
      Have power to cast out Satan?

24   If a kingdom
    Is divided against itself
    That kingdom
    Has no power to stand

25
If a house
Is divided against itself
That house
Has no power to stand

26
If Satan
Stood up against himself
And was divided
He would have no power to stand
But would come to an end

27
For no one
Has the power to enter
A strong man's house
To plunder his goods
Unless he first ties up
The strong man
And then he will plunder
His house

28
Certainly I say to you
That the sons of men
Will be freed from all sins
And from blasphemies
However they may blaspheme
29
But whoever blasphemes
Against the Holy Spirit
Will not be forgiven
Throughout the ages
But is guilty of sin
Unto the ending of time

30 This was because they had said
   He has an unclean spirit

The family of Jesus
31 His mother
   And his brothers
   Came and stood outside
   And sent to call him

32 But a crowd
   Was sitting round him
      So when they said to him
         See how your mother
         And your brothers
         And your sisters
         Are outside
         Looking for you

33   He answered them
            Who is my mother
            And who are my brothers?

34   Looking round
         At those sitting in the circle
         He said
            See here my mother
            And my brothers

35   Whoever does the will of God
        Is my brother
        And my sister
        And my mother

4   *The parable of the sower*
1   Again
        When he began to teach
        Beside the sea
        Such a great crowd surrounded him
        That he embarked in a boat
        And sat in it
        Out on the water
        While all the crowd remained on land
        By the sea shore

2   He taught them many things
        In parables
        And when he was teaching
            He said
3   Now listen
                See how a sower
                Went out to sow

4   And it happened
                That as he sowed
                Some seed
                Fell beside the path
                Then came the birds
                And ate it up

5   Other seed
       Fell in rocky places
       Where it did not have much earth
       And sprouted immediately
       Because it had no depth of earth
6   When the sun rose
       It was scorched
       And as it had no root
       It withered

7   Other seed
       Fell among the thorn bushes
       As the thorns came up
       They choked it
       And it yielded no fruit

8   Other seed
       Fell into cultivated ground
       It sprouted and grew
       And yielded fruit
       Increased thirty times
       Sixty times
       And a hundred times

9   Then he said
       Whoever has ears to hear
       Should hear

10   When he was on his own
Others who were round him
With the twelve
Asked about the parables

11   He said to them
The mystery
Of the kingdom of God
Has been given to you
But for those outside
Everything is in parables

12   *That seeing*
They may see and not perceive
That hearing
They may hear and not understand
Lest they might turn again
And be forgiven

13   And he said to them
If you do not see the meaning
Of this parable
Then how will you understand
All other parables?

14   The sower sows the word

15   Those are the ones
Where the word is sown
Beside the path
When they hear it

Satan comes immediately
And takes away the word
Which was sown in them

16 Those are also the ones
Where it is sown
In the rocky places
When they hear the word
They immediately receive it with joy
17 But having no root in themselves
It is short-lived
When difficulties come about
Or there is persecution
Because of the word
They give up at once

18 Others are the ones
Where it is sown
Among the thorn bushes
The ones who hear the word
19 Then the problems of the times
The enticement of riches
And all other passionate desires
Strangle the word
And it yields no fruit

20 Those are the ones
Where it is sown
On the cultivated ground
Who on hearing the word
Welcome it

And yield fruit
Increased thirty times
Sixty times
And a hundred times

Jesus teaches in parables

21 And he said to them
The lamp
Is not brought in
To be put under the corn measure
Or under the bed
But on the lampstand

22 For nothing is secret
Except to be revealed
Nor was concealed
Except to be made visible

23 Whoever has ears to hear
Should hear

24 And he said to them
See that you listen

With the measure you measure
It will be measured to you
And more will be added to you

25 Whoever has
More will be a gift to him

And whoever has not
Even what he has
Will be taken from him

26   And he said
The kingdom of God
Is like this

As if a man
Should throw the seed
On to the earth
27   And should sleep
And after each night
Rise for the day

Meanwhile the seed
prouts and grows
He does not know how

28   Of its own accord
The earth bears fruit
First the blade
Then an ear
Then full corn in the ear

29   But when the grain is ready
Immediately he sends out the sickle
Because the harvest has come

30   And he said
To what should we compare

The kingdom of God?
Or what parable should we use?

31   It is like a mustard seed
     When it is sown
     On to the earth
     It is smaller
     Than all the seeds
     On the earth

32   But when it is sown
     And comes up
     It grows taller
     Than all other herbs

     And puts out
     Such large branches
     That the birds of heaven
     Are able to nest in their shade

33 In many such parables
   He spoke the word to them
   As far as they had the ability
   To hear it

34 And he only spoke to them
   In parables
   But when they were by themselves
   He explained everything
   To his own disciples

The calming of the storm

35 On that day
When the evening had come
    Jesus said to them
        Let us cross over
        To the other side

36 They left the crowd
And just as he was
They took him into the boat
And other boats
Went with them

37 There came a gale of wind
And the waves
Crashed into the boat
So that it was now filled

38 But Jesus
Was in the stern
Asleep on a pillow

They woke him
    And said to him
        Teacher
        Does it not matter to you
        That we are lost?

39 On waking
    He spoke sternly to the wind
    And said to the sea

        Be still
        Be silent

    The wind dropped
    And there was a great calm

40   And he said to them
                Why are you such cowards?
                Have you no faith?

41   They were terribly afraid
            And said to one another
                Who is this
                That both the wind
                And the sea
                Obey him?

5   *The healing of the man with legion*
1   On the other side of the sea
      They came to the district of the Gadarenes

2   As Jesus disembarked from the boat
      There met him a man
      Who came out from among the tombs
      And who had an unclean spirit.

3   He housed among the tombs
      And no longer did anyone
      Have the power
      To bind him with a chain

4   As he had often been found
With fetters and chains
And he had burst the chains
And broken the fetters
And no one was strong enough
To subdue him

5   He was always among the tombs
And in the mountains
Crying out night and day
And cutting himself with stones

6   When he saw Jesus
From a long way off
He ran and worshipped him

7   And crying out in a loud voice
He said
What is there between me and you
Jesus
Son of the most high God?
Swear by God
Not to torment me

8   Because he had said
To the unclean spirit
That he should come out of the man

9   And Jesus asked him the question
What is your name?

He said to him
    My name is Legion
    Because we are many

10   And he implored him earnestly
Not to send them
Out of the district

11   A large herd of pigs
Was feeding there
On the mountain side

12   The unclean spirits implored him
Saying
    Send us into the pigs
    So that we may go into them

13   And he allowed them to go

They came out
And went into the pigs
And the whole herd
Rushed headlong down the steep incline
Into the sea
There were about two thousand
And they were drowned in the sea

14   The herdsmen fled
And reported it in the town
And in the countryside

Then the people came out
To see what had happened

15 When they came to Jesus
And observed the demoniac
The one who had the Legion
Sitting clothed
And come to his senses
They were afraid

16 Those who had seen it
Told the story of what had happened
To the demoniac
And about the pigs

17 Then they began to beg Jesus
To leave their territory

18 As he embarked in the boat
The one
Who had been possessed by demons
Begged to go with him

19 He did not permit this
     But said to him
          Go to your house
          And to your people
          And tell them
          How the Lord pitied you
          And what he has done for you

20 He went away
And began to proclaim
Throughout the Decapolis
What Jesus had done for him
And every one was astonished

The cure of a woman and raising Jairus' daughter
21 When Jesus
Had crossed over again in the boat
And come to the other side
Crowds had gathered to meet him

He was beside the sea
22 When one of the leaders of the synagogue
Came to him
His name was Jairus
And when he saw Jesus
He fell at his feet

23 And imploring him insistently
He said
My little daughter
Is at the end
Come and lay your hands on her
So that she may be saved
And live

24 Jesus went with him
And a large crowd followed
Hemming him in

25 There was a woman
Who had suffered from severe bleeding
For twelve years

26 She had been treated
By a great many doctors
And spent all that she possessed
But nothing had helped
It had rather become worse

27 Because she had heard about Jesus
She came behind him in the crowd
And touched his cloak

28   As she said
        If I even touch his cloak
        I shall be saved

29 Instantly
The flow of her blood dried up
And she was aware in her body
That she was cured of her affliction

30 As Jesus
Knew at once within himself
That power
Had gone forth from him
He turned round in the crowd
    And said
        Who touched my cloak?

31   His disciples said to him
          You see the crowd jostling you
          And yet you say
          Who touched me?

32   Then he looked round
      To see who had done this

33   The woman
      Came in fear and trembling
      As she was aware
      Of what had happened to her
      She fell down in front of him
      And told him all the truth

34   And he said to her
              Daughter
              Your faith has saved you
              Go in peace
              And be cured of your affliction

35   While he was still speaking
      Some people
      Came from the leader's house
          Saying
              Your daughter has died
              Why do you trouble the Teacher?

36   But Jesus overheard
      What they were saying
          And he said

To the leader of the synagogue
   Do not be afraid
   Only have faith

37 And he allowed no one
To go with him
Except Peter and James
And John the brother of James

38 They came into Jairus's house
And Jesus observed a great commotion
With weeping
And crying out loud

39   As he went in
   He said to them
      Why do you make so much noise
      And weep?
      The child has not died
      She is sleeping

40 They laughed at him
But he put them all outside

Then he took the child's father
And her mother
Also those who were with him
And went in where the child was

41 He took hold of the child's hand
   And said to her

Talitha cumi
(Which is translated
Young girl
I say to you
Get up)

42 At once
The young girl rose up
And walked

She was twelve years old

At that moment
They were quite overcome with
    bewilderment

43 But Jesus
Gave strict orders that no one
Should be made aware of it
And told them
To give her something to eat

6 *Jesus is not accepted in his native place*
1   On going away from there
He went to his native place
And his disciples followed him

2   When the sabbath came
He began to teach in the synagogue

Many of those who heard him
Were astonished
And said
Where does he get all this?
And what is the wisdom
Which is given to him?
How are such powerful deeds
Performed through his hands?

3   Is he not the carpenter
The son of Mary
The brother of James and Joses
And of Judas and Simon?
Are not his sisters
Here with us?

And they would not accept him

4   Jesus said to them
A prophet
Is not without honour
Except in his native place
Among his kinsmen
And in his own house

5   There
He was unable
To perform any powerful deeds
Only laying his hands
On a few sick people

He healed them
6 And he wondered at their lack of faith

Then he went about
Teaching in turn among the villages

The mission of the twelve
7 He called the twelve
To come to him
And began to send them out
Two by two
And gave them authority
Over the unclean spirits

8 He instructed them
To take nothing for the road
Except for a staff
Neither bread nor bag
Nor small coins in their belt
9 They should wear sandals with straps
But not put on two tunics

10 And he said to them
Wherever
You go into a house
Stay until you leave that place
11 And wherever
They do not receive you
Or hear you
When you go out

62

> Shake off the dust under your feet
> As a witness to them

12 They went out
Preaching a change of heart and mind
13 They cast out many demons
And anointing with oil
Many who were sick
They healed them

The death of John the Baptist
14 King Herod heard this
Because Jesus' name
Had become well known

> There were some who said
> John
> The one baptizing
> Has been raised from the dead
> Therefore these powerful deeds
> Are active in him

15 Others said
He is Elijah

> While others said
> He is a prophet
> Like one of the prophets

16 But when he heard this
Herod said

John
Whom I
I beheaded
Has been raised

17 For Herod
Had himself sent to take John
And held him bound in prison
Because of Herodias
The wife of his brother Philip
Whom he had married

18 As John
Had told Herod
That it was not lawful
For him to have his brother's wife

19 Now Herodias
Was angry with him
And wished to kill him
But she had not the power

20 Because Herod
Was afraid of John
As he knew
That he was a just and holy man
And kept a watch on him

When he heard him
He was greatly disturbed
Yet he was pleased to hear him

21   A suitable day came
      When Herod
      To celebrate his birthday
      Gave a supper for his courtiers
      The commanding officers
      And the chief men of Galilee

22   When the daughter of Herodias
      Came in herself and danced
      She pleased Herod
      And those at the table with him

          Then the king
          Said to the young girl
              Ask whatever you wish
              And I will give it to you

23   And he vowed to her
              I will give you
              Whatever you ask
              Even half of my kingdom

24   She went out
          And said to her mother
              What am I to ask?

          She answered
              The head of John
              The one who baptizes

25 At once
  She came swiftly
  Into the king's presence
   And asked
    I wish you to give me immediately
    A dish with the head
    Of John the Baptist

26 The king became deeply distressed
  But because of his oaths
  And those at the table with him
  He did not wish
  To break faith with her

27 Straight away
  The king sent an executioner
  With orders to bring his head

  He went and beheaded him
  In the prison
28 And brought his head on a dish
  And gave it to the young girl
  And the girl
  Gave it to her mother

29 When his disciples heard it
  They came and took his dead body
  And put it in a tomb

The feeding of the five thousand

30 The Apostles
Gathered again to Jesus
And gave him news
Of all that they had done
And had taught

31   He said to them
        Come away by yourselves
        To a desert place
        And rest a short while

For so many
Were coming and going
They did not even
Have the opportunity to eat

32 They embarked in the boat
And went away by themselves
To a desert place

33 Many people saw them going
And recognized them
So they came from all the towns
And running together on foot
Reached the place before them

34 When Jesus landed
He saw a large crowd
And had compassion on them
Because they were like sheep

67

Without a shepherd
And he began to teach them
About many things

35 As the hour grew late
    His disciples came to him
    And said
        This is a desert place
        And now the hour is late
36   Send them away
        So that they may disperse
        To the farms and villages round about
        And buy themselves
        What they need to eat

37 But he answered them
    You give them
    Something to eat

So they said to him
    Shall we go away
    And spend two hundred denarii
    On bread
    And give it to them to eat?

38 And he said to them
    How many loaves have you?
    Go and see

When they had discovered
    They said

Five
And two fish

39 He ordered them
To sit down for a meal
In companies together
On the green grass

40 So they sat down in squares
Of a hundred
And of fifty

41 He took the five loaves
And the two fishes
And looking up to heaven
He said a blessing

He broke the loaves
And gave them to the disciples
To serve out to the people
And the two fish
He divided among them all

42 They all ate
And were satisfied

43 And they took up
Twelve wicker baskets full of pieces
Including fragments from the fish

44   Those who had eaten the loaves
     Were five thousand men

45   Then he demanded that his disciples
     Should embark at once in the boat
     And go ahead of him to Bethsaida
     On the other side
     While he sent the crowd away

46   After he had taken leave of them
     He went on to the mountain
     To pray

Jesus comes to the disciples on the sea
47   When evening came
     The boat
     Was in the midst of the sea
     And he was alone
     On the land

48   When he saw
     That they were having difficulty in rowing
     Because the wind was against them
     He came to them
     At about the fourth watch of the night
     Walking on the sea
     And would have passed by them

49   But as they saw him
     Walking on the sea
     They thought that it was a phantom

And cried out
50 Because they all saw him
And were troubled

    But he spoke to them at once
    And said
      Be brave
      I
      I AM
      Do not be afraid

51 Then he came into the boat
With them
And the wind dropped

Inwardly
They were filled with the greatest awe
52 Because they did not understand
About the loaves
As their hearts and minds
Were not open

Healings at Gennesaret
53 They crossed over
And reached the land at Gennesaret
Where they cast anchor

54 As they disembarked out of the boat
The people recognized him
55 And at once
They began to run around

All that countryside
Carrying round the sick on their mats
When they heard where he was

56 And wherever he went
Whether into the villages
Or into the towns
Or in the countryside
They brought the invalids
Into the open spaces
And begged him to allow them
To touch even the border of his cloak
And all who touched him
Were saved

7 *A discussion about tradition*
1 When the Pharisees
And some of the scribes
Who had come from Jerusalem
Were gathered round him
2 They saw some of his disciples
Eating with unclean hands
That is
Eating bread without having washed

3 Because the Pharisees
And indeed all the Jews
Do not eat
Unless they have first washed their hands
As they keep the tradition of the elders
4 When they come from the market

They do not eat
Without having first cleansed themselves

And there are many other things prescribed
Such as
How cups and utensils and copper pans
Should be washed

5   The Pharisees and the scribes
Asked him
    Why do your disciples
    Not follow the tradition of the elders
    But eat bread
    With unclean hands?

6   And Jesus said to them
    It was right
    What Isaiah prophesied
    About you hypocrites
    The people
    Honour me with their lips
    But their heart
    Is far from me
7   *They worship me in vain*
    Teaching as doctrine
    The commandments of men

8   You leave
    The commandments of God
    And hold fast
    The tradition of men

9   And he said to them
                You succeed in setting aside
                The commandments of God
                So that you may keep
                Your own tradition
10   For Moses said
                Honour your father and your mother
                Whoever speaks evil
                Of father or mother
                Let him end in death

11   But you
                You say that if a man
                Declares to his father or mother
                The help
                Which I would have given to you
                Is Korban
                Which means a gift to God
12   You no longer
                Allow him to do anything
                For his father or mother

13   Thus you annul the word of God
                By your tradition
                Which you received
                As indeed you do many such things

Clean and unclean
14   Calling the crowds to him again
                He said to them

Listen all of you
And understand

15   There is nothing
        Which enters into a man
        From outside
        Which has the power
        To make him unclean
        But it is those things
        Which come out of a man
        Which make him unclean

[16]

17   When he left the crowds
        And went into a house
        His disciples questioned him
        About the parable

18 And he said to them
        Are you
        You also without understanding?
        Do you not grasp
        That anything
        Which enters into a man
        From outside
        Has no power
        To make him unclean?

19   Because it does not enter his heart
        But his stomach
        And passes out into the drain
        Making all foods clean

20   And he said
       Those things
       Which come out of a man
       Make a man unclean

21   For from within
       Out of the hearts of men
       Come forth the evil thoughts
       Fornications and thefts and murders
22   Adulteries and greed and wickedness
       Deceit and indecency and envy
       Blasphemy and arrogance and folly
23   All these evil things
       Coming forth from within
       Make a man unclean

The healing of the Syrophoenician woman's daughter
24 Going up from there
Jesus went away
Into the district of Tyre

He went into a house
And wished no one
To be aware of it
But he could not be kept hidden

25 Straight away
A woman heard about him
Whose daughter had an unclean spirit
So she came
And fell at his feet

26 She was a Greek
By birth a Syrophoenician

And she asked him
To cast the demon
Out of her daughter

27 And he said to her
First allow the children
To be satisfied
As it is not right
To take the children's bread
And to throw it to the house-dogs

28 She answered him
Yes Lord
But the house-dogs under the table
Eat the children's crumbs

29 And he said to her
Because of what you have said
Go
The demon has left your daughter

30 When she went away
To her house
She found the child
Laid on the bed
And the demon gone

The healing of the deaf man

31 Again leaving the district of Tyre
He came through Sidon
To the Sea of Galilee
Passing through the district
Of the Decapolis

32 They brought someone to him
Who was deaf
And had difficulty in speaking
And they begged him
To put his hand on him

33 Taking him on his own
Away from the crowds
He put his fingers into his ears
And spat and touched his tongue
34 Looking up to heaven
He groaned
And said to him
Ephphatha
(Which means
Be opened)

35 His ears were opened
And at once
The bond of his tongue
Was loosened
And he spoke clearly

36   Jesus ordered them
To tell no one
But the more insistent he was
The more widely
They made it known

37   They were extremely astonished
    And said
        He has done everything well
        He makes both the deaf hear
        And the dumb speak

8 *The feeding of the four thousand*
1   During those days
Large crowds collected again
And they did not have anything to eat

2   Jesus called his disciples to him
    And said to them
        I have compassion on the people
        Because they have been with me
        For three days
        And do not have anything to eat
3   If I send them away to their homes
        Without food
        They will faint on the road
        For some of them
        Have come from far away

4   His disciples answered him
    Where could anyone

79

Get enough bread
To satisfy them
Here in a desert place

5   He asked them
How many loaves
Have you?

And they said
Seven

6   He ordered the people
To sit down on the ground
And taking the seven loaves
He gave thanks
And broke them

He gave them to his disciples
To serve out
And they served the people

7   They had a few little fish
And he blessed them
And told his disciples
To serve them also

8   They ate and were satisfied
And they collected the fragments left over
In seven reed baskets

9 Now there were about four thousand
And he sent them away

The Pharisees seek for a sign
10 At once
He embarked in the boat
With his disciples
And went to the district of Dalmanutha

11 The Pharisees came out
And began to debate with him
Seeking from him
A sign from heaven
In order to test him

12 Groaning deeply in his spirit
He said
Why does this generation
Seek a sign?
Certainly I say to you
No sign
Will be given to this generation

The disciples fail to understand the signs
13 Leaving them again
He embarked
And went to the other side

14 His disciples
Had forgotten to take bread

And had only one loaf
With them in the boat

15 And he spoke to them severely
Saying
See that you take no notice
Of the yeast of the Pharisees
Or the yeast of the Herodians

16 They decided among themselves
That it was because
They had no bread

17 As he was aware of this
He said
Why have you decided
That it is because
You have no bread?
Do you still not grasp
Or understand?
Are your hearts and minds closed?

18 *Although you have eyes*
Do you not see?
Although you have ears
Do you not hear?
And do you not remember?

19 When I broke the five loaves
For the five thousand
How many wicker baskets

Full of fragments
Did you take up?

They said to him
Twelve

20 When the seven
For the four thousand
How many reed baskets
With the quantity of fragments
Did you take up?

And they said
Seven

21 And he said to them
Do you still not understand?

The healing of a blind man
22 They came to Bethsaida
And some of the people
Brought to him a blind man
And they begged him to touch him

23 Taking the blind man
By the hand
He led him away
Out of the village

Then he spat on his eyes
And putting his hands on him

83

He asked him
>Do you see anything?

24 Looking up
He said
>I see men
>They are like trees
>That I observe walking

25 Again
He put his hands
On his eyes
And as he looked steadily
His sight was restored
And he saw everything distinctly

26 Jesus sent him to his house
And said
>You should not go into the village

Peter declares Jesus to be the Christ
27 Jesus went out with his disciples
To the villages of Caesarea Philippi
And on the road
>He questioned his disciples
>Saying to them
>>Whom do men believe me to be?

28 And they answered him
>John the Baptist
>And others Elijah

84

But others say
One of the prophets

29 He asked them
But you
Whom do you believe me to be?

Peter answered him
You are the Christ

30 And he warned them
To tell no one about him

31 He began to teach them
That it is necessary
For the Son of Man
To have great suffering
And be rejected by the elders
The chief priests
And the scribes
To be killed
And after three days
To rise again

32 He said this openly
And Peter took him aside
And began to speak sternly to him

33 But he turned
And seeing his disciples
He spoke sternly to Peter

And said
>Get behind me
>Satan
>Because you are not thinking
>Of the concerns of God
>But of the concerns of men

Following Christ
34 He called the crowd to him
With his disciples
>And said to them
>>If anyone
>>Has the will to come after me
>>He should not consider himself
>>But take his cross
>>And follow me

35 >>For whoever wishes to save
>>His soul-bearing life
>>Will lose it
>>But whoever will lose
>>His soul-bearing life
>>For my sake
>>And the Gospel
>>Will save it

36 >>What use is it to a man
>>To gain the whole world
>>And suffer the loss
>>Of his living soul

37   What could a man give
          As the price
          Of his living soul?

38   For whoever
          Is ashamed of me
          And of my words
          In this false and sinful
              generation
          The Son of Man
          Will be ashamed of him
          When he comes
          Revealing the glory of his Father
          With the holy angels

9   And he said to them
              Certainly I say to you
              That there are some standing here
              Who will surely not taste death
              Until they see the Kingdom of God
              Come with power

The Transfiguration
2   After six days
      Jesus
      Took Peter and James and John
      And brought them up
      On to a high mountain
      Alone by themselves

He was transformed
In their presence
3 And his clothing
Became shimmering white
Very white like snow
Such as no fuller on the earth
Would be able to whiten

4 And there appeared to them
Elijah with Moses
Conversing with Jesus

5   Peter said to Jesus
        Rabbi
        It is right for us to be here
        Let us put up three tents
        One for you
        One for Moses
        And one for Elijah

6 He did not know
How he answered
As they were desperately afraid

7 And there came a cloud
Which overshadowed them
    And a voice
    Came out of the cloud
        This is my Son
        The beloved
        Hear him

8   Suddenly
     As they looked round
     They no longer saw anyone
     Except only Jesus with them

9   Coming down from the mountain
     He ordered them
     Not to tell anyone
     The story of what they had seen
     Until the Son of Man
     Should have risen from the dead

10   So they kept it close among themselves
     As he had said
     Discussing what that is
     To rise from the dead

11   They asked him
             Why do the scribes
             Say that Elijah must come first?

12   And he said to them
             Indeed Elijah comes first
             And will restore everything
             For what has been written
             About the Son of Man
             Except that he should suffer
             And be despised?

13   But I say to you
             That Elijah has come

89

And they treated him
Just as they wished
As it has been written about him

The healing of a boy with a dumb spirit

14 When they came to the disciples
They saw a large crowd round them
And scribes discussing with them

15 Immediately
When the people saw Jesus
They were greatly astonished
And came running to greet him

16 He asked them
    What are you discussing with them?

17 And one of the crowd
Answered him
    Teacher
    I have brought my son to you
    As he has a dumb spirit
18 And wherever it seized him
    It tears him
    And he foams at the mouth
    And grinds his teeth
    He is wasting away
    And when I asked your disciples
    To cast it out
    They had not the strength

19   Jesus answered them
           O generation without faith
           How long
           Shall I be with you?
           How long
           Shall I endure you?
           Bring him to me

20   They brought him to Jesus

When the spirit saw him
At once it threw the boy down
Who fell on the earth
And rolled there
Foaming at the mouth

21   Jesus asked his father
           For how long a time
           Has this been happening to him?

And he said
           From childhood
22   And often
           It threw him into the fire
           And into the water
           To destroy him
           But if you have the power
           To do anything to help us
           Have compassion on us

23   Jesus said to him
        You say
        If you have the power
        Whoever has faith
        Has the power to do anything

24   The child's father
    Cried out at once
    In tears
        I do believe
        May you help my lack of faith

25 When Jesus
Saw that a crowd
Came running together
    He spoke sternly to the unclean spirit
    And said to it
        Dumb and deaf spirit
        I
        I command you
        To come forth out of him
        And you may never
        Enter him again

26 Shouting
And throwing him down violently
It came out
Leaving him as if dead
So that many people said
That he had died

27   But Jesus
      Took hold of his hand
      And lifted him
      And he rose up

28   Then Jesus went into a house
      And when his disciples
      Were alone with him
          They asked him
              Why did we not have power
              To cast it out?

29   And he told them
              Nothing gives power
              To cast out this sort
              Except prayer

Teaching the disciples in Galilee and Capernaum
30   They went away from there
      And passed through Galilee

      He did not wish
      That anyone should be aware of it
31   As he was teaching his disciples
          Saying to them
              The Son of Man
              Will be betrayed
              Into the hands of men
              And they will kill him
              Three days after being killed
              He will rise up

32 They did not understand
What he said
And were afraid to question him

33 They came to Capernaum
When they were in the house
He asked them
What were you discussing
On the road?

34 They were silent
As on the road
They had been discussing
Who was the greatest

35 He sat down
And calling the twelve
He said to them
If anyone wishes to be first
He shall be last of all
And be the server of all

36 Then he took a child
And placed him in among them

Taking him in his arms
He said to them
37 Whoever receives
One of such children
In my name
Receives me

And whoever receives me
Does not receive me
But the one who sent me

38 John said to him
Teacher
We saw someone
Casting out demons in your name
Who does not follow us
And because he does not follow us
We forbade him

39 But Jesus said
Do not forbid him
For there is no one
Who does powerful work
In my name
And who will soon be able
To speak evil of me

40 He who is not against us
Is for us

41 Whoever gives you
A cup of water to drink
In the name of Christ
To whom you belong
Certainly I say to you
By no means
Will he lose his reward

42   Whoever causes the downfall
Of one of these little ones
Who believe in me
It would be right
For him to have a great millstone
Hung round his neck
And to be thrown into the sea

43   If your hand
Causes your downfall
Cut it off
It is right for you to enter maimed
Into Life
Rather than having two hands
To go into the burning rubbish
Into the fire
Which cannot be put out

[44]
45   If your foot
Causes your downfall
Cut it off
It is right for you to enter lame
Into Life
Rather than having two feet
To be thrown into the burning
    rubbish

[46]
47   If your eye
Causes your downfall
Pluck it out
It is right for you to enter one-eyed

Into the kingdom of God
Rather than having two eyes
To be thrown into the burning
   rubbish

48 *Where their worm does not die*
And the fire is never put out

49 For everyone
Will be salted with fire
And every sacrifice
Will be salted with salt

50 Salt is useful
But if the salt becomes saltless
How will you season it?
Have salt in yourselves
And be at peace with one another

10 *A discussion about divorce*

1 He left there
And went up into Judea
Into the territory beyond the Jordan

Again
Crowds went with him
And again
He taught them
As was his custom

2 Some Pharisees came up to him
Asking him

In order to test him
Whether it is lawful
For a man to release a wife

3   He answered them
         What did Moses command you?

4   They said
         Moses
         Allowed a written document of
            divorce
         For her release

5   But Jesus said to them
         It was for your unyielding hearts
         That he wrote you this
            commandment

6   From the beginning of creation
         They were made male and female

7   Because of this
         A man shall leave
         His father and mother
         And be united with his wife
8   *And the two shall be one flesh*
         So that they are no longer two
         But one flesh

9   What God
         Joined together

Man
Should not separate

10 When they were in the house
The disciples
Questioned him again about this

11 He said to them
Whoever releases his wife
And marries another
Commits adultery with her
12 And if she releases her husband
And marries another
She commits adultery

Children are brought to Jesus
13 They brought children to him
So that he might touch them
But the disciples reproved them

14 When Jesus saw this
He was indignant
And said to them
Allow the children
To come to me
Do not hinder them
For as they are
So is the kingdom of God

15 Certainly I say to you
Whoever does not receive

The kingdom of God
As does a child
There is no doubt
That he shall not enter into it

16   And taking them in his arms
He blessed them
Putting his hands on them

The rich man

17   As he set out on the road
Someone came running up to him
And kneeling in front of him
    Asked him
      Good Teacher
      What shall I do
      To inherit life
      Throughout the ages

18   Jesus said to him
      Why do you call me good?
      No one is good
      Except God only

19   You know the commandments
      Do not kill
      Do not commit adultery
      Do not steal
      Do not witness falsely
      Do not cheat
      Honour your father and your mother

20   He answered him
            Teacher
            I have kept all this
            From my youth

21   But Jesus gazing into him
     Loved him
            And said
                 There is still something wanting
                 Go and sell what you have
                 And give it to the poor
                 Then you will have treasure in heaven
                 And come
                 Follow me

22   He was downcast
     At what was said
     And went sadly away
     As he had extensive possessions

23   Looking round
        Jesus said to his disciples
                 How difficult it will be
                 For those who have riches
                 To enter the kingdom of God

24   The disciples
     Were astounded at his words

            Jesus said to them again
                 Children

How difficult it is
To enter the kingdom of God

25   It is easier for a camel
To go through the eye of a needle
Than for one who is rich
To enter the kingdom of God

26   They were absolutely astonished
And said to one another
Then who
Is able to be saved?

27   Gazing into them
Jesus said
With men it is impossible
But not with God
For with God
All things are possible

28   Peter began to say to him
You see
How we have left everything
And followed you

29   Jesus said
Certainly I say to you
There is no one
Who has left house
Or brothers or sisters
Or mother or father

Or children or lands
For my sake
And for the Gospel
30   But will receive a hundred times more
Houses
And brothers and sisters
And mothers and children
And lands
With persecutions
Now at this season
And in the time to come
Life throughout the ages

31   But many that are first
Will be last
And the last first

The last prophecy of the Passion
32   They were on the road
Going up to Jerusalem
And Jesus
Was leading them on

They were astounded
And those following
Were afraid
As taking the twelve again
    He began to tell them
    What was about to happen to him
33   Now see
        How we are going up to Jerusalem

And the Son of Man
Will be betrayed
To the chief priests
And to the scribes

They will condemn him
To death
And will deliver him
To the Gentiles
34   They will mock him
And spit on him
They will scourge him
And kill him
And after three days
He will rise

The request of James and John

35   James and John
The sons of Zebedee
Came to him and said
    Teacher
    We wish you to do for us
    Whatever we ask

36   He said to them
    What do you wish me
    To do for you?

37   They said to him
    Grant us
    That we may sit

One on your right
And one on your left
In your glory

38 But Jesus said to them
You do not know
What you ask
Are you able to drink the cup
Which I myself drink
Or to be baptized with the baptism
With which I
I am baptized?

39 They said to him
We are able

Jesus said to them
You shall drink the cup
Which I myself drink
And be baptized with the baptism
With which I
I am baptized
40 But to sit on my right
Or on my left side
Is not mine to give
But is for those
For whom it has been prepared

41 When the ten heard this
They began to be indignant
About James and John

42   Jesus called them to him
And said
    You know
    That those who think to rule the
        Gentiles
    Dominate them
    And their great ones
    Have authority over them

43   But it is not so
    Among you
    For whoever wishes to become great
    Among you
    Shall be your server

44   And whoever wishes to be first
    Among you
    Shall be the servant of all
45   For even the Son of Man
    Did not come to be served
    But to serve
    And to give his soul-bearing life
    As a ransom for many

The healing of blind Bartimaeus
46   They came to Jericho
And as he left Jericho
With his disciples
And a considerable crowd
A blind beggar

Bartimaeus
The son of Timaeus
Was sitting at the side of the road

47 When he heard
That it was Jesus of Nazareth
He began to shout
Jesus
Son of David
Pity me

48 Many ordered him to be quiet
But he shouted all the more
Son of David
Pity me

49 Jesus stood still
And said
Call him

And they called the blind man
Saying to him
Courage
Get up
He is calling you

50 So he threw off his cloak
And leaping up
He came to Jesus

51 Jesus asked him
> What do you wish me
> To do for you?

The blind man said to him
> Rabboni
> That I may see again

52 Jesus said to him
> Go
> Your faith has saved you

Immediately
He could see again
And followed him
On the road

11 *The entry into Jerusalem*
1 When they came near Jerusalem
To Bethphage and Bethany
On the Mount of Olives
He sent out two of his disciples
2 > Saying to them
> > Go into the village in front of you
> > And immediately you come into it
> > You will find a colt tied up
> > On which no man has yet sat
> > Untie it and bring it

3
       If anyone says to you
       Why are you doing this?
       Say
       The Lord needs it
       And will send it here again
       At once

4
They went and found a colt
Tied at a door
Outside in the street
And they untied it

5
       Some of the people standing there
       Said to them
           What are you doing
           Untying the colt?

6
They answered
As Jesus had told them
And they let them go

7
They brought the colt to Jesus
And threw their cloaks on it
And he sat on it

8
Many
Spread out their cloaks on the road
And others
A covering of greenery
Which they cut from the fields

9 Those who went in front
And those who followed
    Cried out
        Hosanna
        Blest be the one who comes
        In the name of the Lord
10   Blest be the coming kingdom
        Of our father David
        Hosanna
        In the highest places

11 He entered Jerusalem
And went into the Temple
Where he looked round at everything
And as the hour was now late
He went out to Bethany
With the twelve

The fig tree and the clearing of the Temple
12 On the next day
As they went out of Bethany
He was hungry
13 And seeing in the distance
A fig tree in leaf
He went to it
As perhaps he might find
Something on it

When he came he found
Nothing but leaves
As it was not the season for figs

14   He spoke to it
Saying
     No more
     May anyone eat of your fruit
     Throughout the ages

And the disciples heard him

15   They came to Jerusalem
And entering the Temple
He began to turn out
Those who were selling
And those who were buying
In the Temple

He overturned
The tables of the money-changers
And the seats
Of those selling doves
16   And he did not allow anyone
To carry goods through the Temple

17   And he taught them
     Has it not been written
     My house
     Shall be called a house of prayer
     For all the nations
     But you yourselves
     Have made of it
     A robber's cave

18 The chief priests and the scribes
Heard it
And tried to find a way
To destroy him
As they were afraid of him
Because the crowds
Were all astonished at his teaching

19 When evening came
They left the city

20 As they passed by
Early in the morning
They saw the fig tree
Withered from the roots

21 Peter remembered
And said to him
Rabbi
See how the fig tree
Which you cursed
Has been withered

Teaching about prayer
22 Jesus said to them
Have faith in God
23 Certainly I say to you
Whoever says to this mountain
Be taken up
And thrown into the sea
And does not waver in his heart

112

But believes
That it will happen as he says
Then so it will be for him

24 Therefore I tell you
If you believe that you received
Everything for which you pray
And for which you ask
Then so it will be for you

25 When you stand and pray
If you have anything against anyone
Forgive them
And your Father in the heavens
Will forgive your shortcomings
26 But if you do not forgive
Neither will your Father in the heavens
Forgive your shortcomings

27 Again
They came to Jerusalem

As he walked in the Temple
The chief priests
The scribes
And the elders
28 Came to him and said
By what authority
Are you doing these things?
Or who gave you the authority
Which allows you to do them?

29   Jesus said to them
            I will ask you one question
            Which you must answer me
            Then I will tell you
            By what authority
            I do these things

30   Was the baptism of John
            From heaven
            Or from men?
            You must answer me

31   They discussed it among themselves
            And said
            If we reply
            From heaven
            He will say
            Why then did you not believe him?
32   But what if we reply
            From men?

They were afraid of the crowd
For everyone held that John
Was really a prophet

33   So they answered Jesus
            We do not know

            And Jesus said to them
            Neither will I
            I say to you

By what authority
I do these things

12 *The parable of the cruel farmers*

1   And he began to speak to them
    In parables
        A man planted a vineyard
        He set a hedge round it
        And dug a pit for the wine press
        And built a watch-tower
        Then he let it to farmers
        And went out of the country.

2   When the season came
    He sent a servant to the farmers
    To receive from them
    Some of the fruits of the vineyard

3   They took him
    And beat him
    Then sent him away with nothing

4   Again
    He sent another servant to them
    That one
    They wounded in the head
    And insulted

5   He sent another
    And that one
    They killed

Then many more
Some were beaten
Others were killed

6 He still had one
A beloved son

He sent him to them
As the last
And said
They will respect my son

7 But those farmers
Said to one another
This is the heir
Come
Let us kill him
And the inheritance
Will be ours

8 They took him
And killed him
And threw him out
Outside of the vineyard

9 What
Will the Lord of the vineyard do?
He will come and destroy the farmers
And will give the vineyard to others

10   Do you not read in the Scripture
        The stone
        Which the builders rejected
        Has become the head of the corner
11   *This comes from the Lord*
        And is wonderful in our eyes?

12 Then they tried to take him
    But because they were aware
    That this parable had been for them
    They were afraid of the crowd
    So they left him
    And went away

The Pharisees ask a question about taxes
13 They sent to him
    Some of the Pharisees
    And some of the Herodians
    So that they could catch him
    In what he said

14   They came and said to him
            Teacher
            We know that you tell the truth
            And that no one's position
            Matters to you
            For you do not look
            At the status of men
            But truthfully
            Teach the way of God

Is it lawful or not
To pay the tax to Caesar?
Should we pay it
Or should we not pay it?

15 But knowing their hypocrisy
He said to them
Why do you tempt me?
Bring me a denarius
So that I may see it

16 Then they brought it

He said to them
Of whom is this portrait
And whose is the inscription?

And they told him
It is Caesar's

17 So Jesus said to them
What belongs to Caesar
Give back to Caesar
And to God
What belongs to God
And they were amazed at him

The Sadducees ask a question about resurrection
18 Sadducees
Who say that there is no resurrection
Came to him

To ask a question
And said

19   Teacher
        Moses wrote for us
        That if any man's brother should die
        Leaving behind a wife
        But not leaving a child
        He may take the wife
        And raise up children
        For his brother

20   There were seven brothers
        And the first took a wife
        When he died
        He left no children

21   And the second
        Took her and died
        Not leaving behind any children

        And in the same way
        The third

22   All the seven left no children

        Last of all
        The wife died

23   In the resurrection
        When they rise again
        To which of them

Will she be wife?
For all the seven
Had her as wife

24 Jesus said to them
Is not this where you are wrong
That you do not know the Scriptures
Or the power of God?
25 For when they rise from the dead
They neither marry
Nor are given in marriage
But are like angels
In the heavens

26 But concerning the dead
That they are raised

Have you not read
In the book of Moses
How God spoke to him
At the thorn-bush
Saying
I
The God of Abraham
And God of Isaac
And God of Jacob?

27 He is not God of the dead
But of the living

You are quite wrong

A scribe asks about the commandments

28 One of the scribes approached
And heard the debate
So when he knew that Jesus
Was well able to answer them
He asked him
Which commandment
Is first of all?

29 Jesus answered
This is the first
Hear O Israel
The Lord our God
Is one Lord
30 *And you shall love*
The Lord your God
With all your heart
And with all your soul
And with all your mind
And with all your strength

31 This is the second
You shall love
Your neighbour as yourself

There is no other commandment
Greater than these

32 The scribe said to him
It is right
Teacher

And the truth
When you say
That there is one
And there is no other
Beside him
33   And to love him
With all the heart
And with all the understanding
And with all the strength
And to love
One's neighbour as oneself
Is more
Than all the burnt offerings
And sacrifices

34   When Jesus
Saw that he answered sensibly
He said to him
      You are not far
      From the kingdom of God

And no one dared
To question him further

A warning about the scribes
35   When he was teaching
In the Temple
Jesus said
      How is it
      That the scribes say
      The Christ is the son of David?

122

36   For David himself said
        When in the Holy Spirit
        The Lord
        Said to my Lord
        Sit on my right hand
        Until I put your enemies
        Under your feet

37   As David himself calls him Lord
        How can he be his son?

The vast crowds
Listened to him gladly

38   And in his teaching
        He said
            Pay no attention to the scribes
            Who wish to walk about
            In long robes
            And be greeted
            In the public places
39   Also to have the first seats
            In the synagogues
            And the best places at meals
40   Who eat up
            The inheritance of widows
            And make pretence
            Of long prayers

        They will be judged
        With greater severity

The widow's gift

41 As he sat down opposite the treasury
He observed how the crowds
Threw their money into the treasury
And how many rich men
Threw in a great deal

42 One poor widow came
And threw in
Two of the smallest coins
Which together make up a quadrans

43 He called his disciples to him
And said to them
Certainly I say to you
This poor widow
Has put in more
Than all those others
Who have given to the treasury

44 They have all given
From what they had over
But she
Out of her need
Threw in all that she possessed
Indeed all her living

13 *Jesus prophesies war and persecution*
1 As he went out of the Temple
One of his disciples
Said to him

Teacher
Look at the kind of stones
And the kind of buildings
That are here

2 Jesus said to him
Do you see these great buildings
By no means will stone
Be left upon stone
That will not be thrown down

3 He sat on the Mount of Olives
Opposite the Temple
Then Peter
James
John
And Andrew
Questioned him on their own

4 Tell us
When will this be
And what will be the sign
When all this
Is about to come to an end?

5 So Jesus began to say to them
Watch out that no one misleads you

6 Many will come in my name
Saying
I
I am
And will mislead many people

7
When you hear battles
And hear tell of battles
Do not be disturbed
This must happen
But it is not yet the end

8
Nation will rise against nation
And kingdom against kingdom
In places there will be earthquakes
There will be famines
These are the beginning
Of the pangs of birth

9
Watch out for yourselves
They will hand you over to councils
You will be beaten in synagogues
And will stand
Before governors and kings
For my sake
As a witness to them

10
But first
The Gospel must be preached
To all the nations

11
When they lead you away
To arrest you
Do not be anxious beforehand
About what you will say
But say
Whatever is given to you

In that hour
Because it is not you
Who speaks
But the Holy Spirit

12   And a brother
Will betray a brother to death
And a father
A child
And children
Will rise against parents
And put them to death

13   Everyone will hate you
Because of my name
But the one
Who remains steadfast to the end
Will be saved

14   But when you see
The abomination of desolation
Stand where it should not
Whoever reads
Let him understand
Then those in Judea
Should flee to the mountains

15   Whoever is on the roof
Should not come down
Or go into his house
To take anything out

16   Whoever is in the fields
      Should not turn back
      To take the cloak
      Which he left behind

17   Alas for the woman
      In those days
      Who carries a child in her womb
      Or has one at her breast

18   But pray
      That it may not be in winter
19   Because those will be days
      Of such persecution
      As there has not been
      From the beginning of creation
      Which God created
      Until now
      And indeed may not be again

20   And unless the Lord
      Cut short those days
      No flesh would be saved
      But for the sake of the elect
      Whom he chose
      He cut short those days

21   Then if any one tells you
      Look
      Here is the Christ
      Or there

Do not believe it

22
False Christs
And false prophets
Will rise up
And will perform signs and portents
And if it is possible
Will even mislead the elect

23
But you yourselves
Should watch out
For I have told you
Everything beforehand

The coming of the Son of Man

24
In those days
After the persecution
Then the sun
Will be darkened
And the moon
Will not shed her beams

25
And the stars
Will fall out of heaven
And the powers in the heavens
Will be shaken

26
Then they will perceive
The Son of Man
Coming in clouds
With great power and glory

27   He will send out the angels
And will gather the elect
From the four winds
From the bounds of earth
To the bounds of heaven

28   And learn this parable
From the fig tree

When the branch becomes tender
And puts out leaves
You are aware
That the summer is near

29   So you also
When you see
That these things are happening
Are aware that he is near
At the doors

30   Certainly I say to you
That this generation will not pass
Before all this will happen

31   Heaven and earth
Will pass away
But my words
Will not pass away

32   About that day
Or that hour
No one knows

Neither the angels in heaven
Nor the Son
Only the Father

33   Watch out
Be wakeful
For you do not know
When the moment will be

34   It is as if a man
Going out of the country
On leaving his house
Gives his servants authority
And to each his work
And commands the doorkeeper
To watch

35   Therefore you should watch
As you do not know
When the Lord of the house
Will come
Whether in the evening
Or at midnight
Or at cockrow
Or in the morning

36   As he might come suddenly
And find you sleeping

37   What I say to you
I say to all
Watch

14 *The anointing at Bethany*

1 Now it was two days
Before the Passover
And the Feast of Unleavened Bread
When the chief priests and the scribes
Aimed to take him by stealth
In order to kill him

2 Because they said
Not at the festival
As it might lead to disorder
Among the people

3 As he was in Bethany
In the house of Simon the leper
And was sitting at the table
A woman came
With an alabaster jar
Of valuable ointment of pure nard
She broke the jar
And poured it over his head

4 Now there were some
Who were indignant
Saying to themselves
Why has there been this loss
Of the ointment?

5 For could not this ointment
Have been sold
For more than three hundred denarii
To be given to the poor?

And they were displeased with her

6 But Jesus said
        Leave her
        Why do you make trouble for her?
        It is an honourable deed
        Which she has performed on me

7 The poor
        You always have with you
        And whenever you wish
        You have the means
        To treat them well
        But you do not always have me

8 She has done what she could
        She has anointed my body
          beforehand
        For burial

9 Certainly I say to you
        Wherever this Gospel is preached
        In the whole world
        What she did
        Will also be related
        As a memorial to her

The betrayal
10 Then Judas Iscariot
        One of the twelve

Went to the chief priests
To betray him to them

11   When they heard it
They were glad
And promised to give him money
So he looked for the right moment
To betray him

Preparations for the Passover
12   On the first day of Unleavened Bread
When they sacrificed the passover
    His disciples said to Jesus
      Where do you wish us to go
      So that we may prepare for you
      To eat the passover?

13   He sent out two of his disciples
    Saying to them
      Go into the city
      And a man
      Will meet you
      Who is carrying a jar of water
      Follow him
14   And wherever he goes in
      Tell the master of the house
      The Teacher says
      Where is my guest room
      Where I may eat the passover
      With my disciples?

15
       He will show you
       A large upper room
       Which has been set out ready
       There prepare for us

16
The disciples went out
And came into the city
There they found everything
As he had told them
And they prepared the Passover

The Last Supper

17
In the evening
He came with the twelve

18
As they were eating at the table
    Jesus said
        Certainly I say to you
        One of you
        Will betray me
        One who is eating with me

19
They began to feel sad
    And to say to him
    One by one
        Surely not I?

20
    And he said to them
        It is one of the twelve
        The one who is dipping with me
        Into the same bowl

21   For indeed the Son of Man
Is going
As it has been written about him
But alas for that man
Through whom the Son of Man
Is betrayed
It would be better for that man
If he had not been born

22   As they were eating
He took bread
And blessing it
He broke it
And gave it to them
    And said
        Take this
        It is my body

23   Then he took a cup
And giving thanks
He gave it to them
They all drank from it
24   And he said to them
        This is my blood
        Of the Covenant
        Which is poured out for many

25   Certainly I say to you
        No more will I drink
        Of the fruit of the vine
        Until that day

When I drink it new
In the kingdom of God

26 When they had sung a hymn
They went out
To the Mount of Olives

Jesus foretells Peter's denial
27 Jesus said to them
All of you will give up
Because it is written
I will strike the shepherd
And the sheep will be scattered
28 But after I am raised
I will go before you to Galilee

29 Peter said to him
Even if all give up
Yet not I

30 Jesus said to him
Certainly I say to you
Today
In this night
Before a cock crows twice
You will disown me three times

31 But he protested all the more
If I must die with you
It is certain
That I will not disown you

And they all said the same

Jesus prays at Gethsemane

32 When they came to a place
The name of which was Gethsemane
    He said to his disciples
        Sit here while I pray

33 He took with him
Peter
James
And John
And beginning to be overwhelmed with
  distress
34   He said to them
        My living soul is sorrowful unto
            death
        Stay here and watch

35 Going forward a little way
He fell on the ground
And prayed
That if it were possible
The hour might pass away from him
36   Saying
        Abba
        Father
        With thee everything is possible
        Remove this cup from me
        But not what I

> I will
> But thou

37 When he came
He found them sleeping
> And said to Peter
> > Simon
> > Are you asleep?
> > Had you no strength
> > To watch one hour?
38 > > Watch and pray
> > That you do not come into
> > > temptation
> > Indeed the spirit is eager
> > But the flesh is weak

39 Again
He went away and prayed
Saying the same words

40 Then again
When he came
He found them sleeping
As their eyes had become heavy
And they did not know
How to answer him

41 The third time
> He came and said to them
> > Sleep now and rest
> > It is enough

The hour has come
You see that the Son of Man
Is betrayed into the hands of sinners
42 Get up
Let us go
Look how near is my betrayer

The arrest
43 Immediately
While he was still speaking
Judas
One of the twelve
Arrived with a crowd
With swords and clubs
From the chief priests
The scribes
And the elders

44 The betrayer
Had agreed to give them a signal
Saying
Whoever I kiss
He it is
Take him
And lead him away securely

45 When he came
He went up to him at once
And said
Rabbi

And kissed him warmly

46 Then they laid their hands on him
To take him

47 But one of those
Who were standing there
Drew his sword
And struck the high priest's servant
Taking off his ear

48 Jesus said to them
Have you come out
As if against a robber
To capture me
With swords and clubs?
49 I was with you every day
Teaching in the Temple
And you did not take me
But the Scripture
Should be fulfilled

50 Then they all left him
And fled

51 And accompanying him
Was a young man
Who was wrapped round
With a linen cloth
Over his nakedness

They took hold of him
52 And he left the linen cloth
And fled naked

Jesus before the council
53 They led Jesus away
To the high priest
Where all the chief priests
The elders
And the scribes
Had come together

54 Peter followed him at a distance
Until he was inside the courtyard
Of the high priest
Where he sat with the attendants
And warmed himself in the firelight

55 The chief priests
And all the council
Looked for witnesses against Jesus
To put him to death
But they did not find any

56 There were many false witnesses
Against him
But their witness did not agree

57 Some false witnesses stood up
And said

58   We heard him saying
                      I myself
                      Will overthrow this shrine
                      Made with hands
                      And after three days
                      I will build another
                      Not made with hands

59   But even then
     Their witness did not agree

60   The high priest
     Rose up among them to question Jesus
           And asked him
                Do you not answer
                These witnesses against you?

61   But he was silent
     And did not answer

           The high priest
        Questioned him again
                Are you the Christ
                The Son of the Blessed?

62   Jesus said
                I
                I AM
                And you will see
                The Son of Man
                Sitting on the right of the Power

And coming with the clouds of
heaven

63   The high priest
Tore his tunic and said
Why do we need more witnesses
64   You heard the blasphemy
How does it appear to you?

And they all condemned him to death

65   Some began to spit at him
And to cover his face
And strike him with their fists
Saying to him
    Prophesy

Then the attendants
Took him and slapped him

Peter's denial
66   Peter was below in the courtyard
When one of the high priest's maidservants
67   Came and saw Peter warming himself
    She looked closely at him
    And said
       You were with Jesus
       The Nazarene

68   But he denied it
And said

I neither know
Nor can understand
What you are saying

Then he went outside
Into the forecourt
And a cock crowed

69 The maidservant saw him
    And again
        Began saying to those standing there
            He is one of them

70 But again
   He denied it

After a little while
    Those standing there
    Said to Peter
        It is true
        That you are one of them
        For you are a Galilean

71 He began to curse
        And to swear
            I do not know the man
            Of whom you are speaking

72 Immediately
   A cock crowed a second time

Then Peter remembered the words
Which Jesus had said to him
Before the cock crows twice
You will disown me three times

And upon this
He wept

15 *Jesus before Pilate*

1   As soon as it was dawn
The chief priests
The elders
And the scribes
Together with the whole council
Made their preparations

Then having tied up Jesus
They led him away
And handed him over to Pilate

2   Pilate asked him
Are you
The King of the Jews?

Jesus answered
You say so

3   Then the chief priests
Accused him of many things

4   Again
       Pilate asked him
              Do you not give any answer?
              See how they accuse you
              Of so much

5   But Pilate was astonished
       That Jesus answered nothing more

6   At a festival
       Pilate
       Released to them one prisoner
       For whom they entreated

7   There was a prisoner
       Called Barabbas
       Who had joined those rebels
       Who had committed murder in the rebellion

8   The crowds gathered
       And began to ask Pilate
       To do for them
       As he had usually done

9   Pilate answered them
              Do you wish me
              To release to you
              The King of the Jews?

10   As he was aware
       That it was because of their jealousy

The chief priests
Had handed him over

11 But the chief priests
Roused up the crowd
To have him release to them
Barabbas

12 Again
Pilate said to them
What shall I do
To him
Whom you call
The King of the Jews?

13 Again
They cried out
Crucify him

14 But Pilate said to them
Why
What evil has he done?

They cried out all the more
Crucify him

15 Pilate
Intent on satisfying the crowd
Released for them
Barabbas

Then having had Jesus scourged
He handed him over
To be crucified

Jesus mocked by the soldiers
16 The soldiers led him away
Into the courtyard
That is
Into the praetorium
And called the whole company together

17 They dressed him in purple
And plaiting a thorny crown
They placed it on him

18   Then they began to salute him
              Hail
              King of the Jews!

19 They struck his head
With a reed
And spat at him
And bending their knees
They worshipped him

20 When they had mocked him
They took the purple off him
And put on him his own clothes

Then they led him out
To crucify him

The Crucifixion

21 They pressed a passer-by into service
To carry his cross
He was Simon
A Cyrenian coming from the country
The father of Alexander and Rufus

22 They brought Jesus
To the place called Golgotha
Which means
The place of a skull
23 Where they gave him wine
Mixed with myrrh
But he did not receive it

24 Then they crucified him
And divided his clothing
Throwing dice
As to what each should take

25 It was the third hour
When they crucified him

26 And over him was written
An inscription
It was the accusation against him
THE KING OF THE JEWS

27 With him they crucified two bandits
One on his right
And one on his left

28   So the Scripture was fulfilled
      Which said
      He was numbered
      With those who broke the law

29   The people passing by blasphemed him
            Shaking their heads
            And saying
                  Aha
                  You who would overthrow the shrine
                  And build it in three days
30   Save yourself
                  Come down from the cross

31   The chief priests and scribes
      Also mocked him
            Saying to one another
            He saved others
                  He cannot save himself
32   Let the Christ
                  The King of Israel
                  Come down from the cross
                  So that we may see and believe

      And those crucified with him
      Reproached him

33   When the sixth hour had come
      Darkness came over all the earth
      Until the ninth hour

34   At the ninth hour
        Jesus called out in a loud voice
            Eloi
            Eloi
            Lama sabachthani?
            (Which is translated
            My God
            My God
            Why hast thou forsaken me?)

35   Some of those who stood there
        When they heard it
        Said
            See
            He calls Elijah

36   Then someone ran
    And filling a sponge with vinegar
    Put it on a reed
    And gave it to him to drink
        Saying
            Leave him
            Let us see if Elijah
            Will come to take him down

37   But Jesus
        Let out a loud cry
        And drew his last breath

38 The curtain of the shrine
Was torn in two
From top to bottom

39 When the centurion
Who was standing there facing him
Saw that he thus
Drew his last breath
   He said
      It is true that this man
      Was a Son of God

40 Some women
Were watching from a distance
Among them Mary Magdalene
Salome
And Mary
Mother of the younger James and of Joses
41 Who had followed him and served him
When he was in Galilee
And also many others
Who had come up with him
To Jerusalem

The burial
42 As it was the Day of Preparation
Which is the day before the sabbath
When evening came
43 Joseph of Arimathea
A respected counsellor
Who himself was awaiting

The kingdom of God
Gathered his courage
And going into Pilate
He asked for the body of Jesus

44   Pilate
Wondered if he could already be dead
And calling the centurion
Enquired of him
Whether he had been dead for some time

45   On hearing from the centurion
He granted the dead body
To Joseph

46   He had purchased a length of linen
So taking him down
He wrapped him in the linen
And deposited him in a tomb
Which had been hewn out of the rock

Then he rolled a stone
Against the door of the tomb

47   Mary Magdalene
And Mary
The mother of Jesus
Watched where he had been laid

16 *The women at the tomb*

1   When the sabbath was over
     Mary Magdalene
     Mary the mother of James
     And Salome
     Went to buy spices
     So that when they came
     They could anoint him

2   Very early
     On the first day after the sabbath
     They came to the tomb
     As the sun was rising
3   And said to one another
             Who will roll away the stone for us
             From the door of the tomb?

4   On looking up they observed
     That the great stone
     Had been rolled back

5   Going into the tomb
     They saw a young man
     Clothed in a white robe
     Sitting on the right side
     And they were exceedingly astonished

6   But he said to them
             Do not be so astonished
             You are looking for Jesus
             The Nazarene

155

Having been crucified
He was raised
He is not here
See the place where they laid him

7   Go and tell his disciples
And Peter
That he is going before you
To Galilee
There you will see him
As he told you

8   And they went out
And fled from the tomb
For trembling and bewilderment
Had taken hold of them
And they said nothing to any one
Because they were afraid

The shorter ending
They reported briefly
To Peter and those with him
All that had been commanded them

And after this
Jesus himself sent out through them
From the East as far as the West
Through all the ages
The sacred and imperishable
Message of salvation

The longer ending

9 Having risen early
On the day following the sabbath
He appeared to Mary Magdalene
From whom
He had cast out seven demons

10 She brought the news
To those who had been with him
Who were mourning and weeping

11 When they heard
That he is alive
And she has had sight of him
They did not believe her

12 After this
As two of them
Walked into the country
He appeared to them
In a different form

13 They brought back the news
To the rest
But they did not believe them either

14 Later
He appeared to the eleven
As they sat at table
And he reproached them
For their unbelief

And closed hearts and minds
Because they did not believe
Those who had sight of him
After he had been raised

15   And he said to them
            Go into all the world
            And preach the Gospel
            To all creation

16   Whoever believes
            And is baptized
            Will be saved
            But whoever does not believe
            Will be condemned

17   Those who believe
            Will have signs
            Which accompany them

18   In my name
            They will cast out demons
            And they will speak in new tongues
            They will pick up serpents
            And if they drink any poison
            It will certainly not hurt them
            They will place their hands
            On sick people
            And they will be well

19 Therefore after speaking to them
The Lord Jesus
Was taken up into heaven
And sat on the right of God

20 But they went out
And preached everywhere
The Lord working with them
And confirming the word
With the signs
Which accompanied them

References

1:2   Mal. 3:1
1:3   Isa. 40:3
2.25f Sam.21:6
4:12 Isa. 6:9f.
7:6f Isa. 29:13
7:10 Exod. 20:12; 21:17; Deut. 5:16
8:18 Jer. 5:21; Ezek. 12:2
9:48 Isa. 66:24
9:49 Ezek. 43:24; Lev. 2:13
10:7 Gen. 2:24
11:9 Ps. 118:26

11:17 Isa. 56:7; Jer. 7:11
12:10f Ps. 118:22f
12:26 Exod. 3:6
12:29f Deut. 6:4f.
12:31 Lev. 19:18
12:36 Ps. 110:1
13:14 Dan. 9:27
14:27 Zech. 13:7
15:28 Isa. 53:12
15:34 Ps. 22:1